Connect Instantly:

60 seconds to Likeability, Meaningful Connections, and Hitting It Off with Anyone

By Patrick King
Dating and Social Skills Coach
www.PatrickKingConsulting.com

As a show of appreciation to my readers, I've put together a **FREE TRAINING VIDEO (just enter your email address)** describing the BEST exercise for immediate social and romantic confidence. Click over to watch it now!

Table of Contents

Connect Instantly: 60 seconds to Likeability, Meaningful Connections, and Hitting It Off with Anyone

Introduction

One of my best friends is a guy named Jason that I met through a couple of soccer teammates.

I take my **hobbies** pretty seriously, which meant that I was playing soccer at least five days a week, mostly with the same people. I also take **leisure time** pretty seriously, which meant that we would almost always rally after the game or practice for drinks and dinner – in hindsight, it's probably difficult to determine which part of the night was the true **motivator** for me.

Here's a **secret** that I only told Jason after I'd known him for about a year, and our best friend moniker seemed inevitable and natural.

I absolutely hated him when I first met him.

And it wasn't a slight aversion, a small annoyance, or just a pebble in my shoe.

He made a spectacularly negative impression on me for reasons that I couldn't quite articulate. We had differing views on everything, and he had a way of making it known.

He seemed to loud, boisterous, and inconsiderate to those who he didn't see eye-to-eye with.

I do remember articulating one thought after we parted ways that night, "**That guy sucked.**"

Luckily for **future Patrick** and **future Jason**, we were essentially forced into constant interaction because of my dedication to soccer. Big groups, small groups, it didn't matter. I ended up seeing Jason at least **twice a week** for a series of months, and I did my best to ignore him.

I highly respected my soccer teammates, so at some point I decided to **engage** Jason out of **curiosity** to try to find out what they liked about him.

All social graces and niceties aside, it turned out that we had a mutual love for **fantasy basketball**, which had literally never come up in conversation. This was the difference-maker and gamechanger in how I viewed him, as I could actually ignore my negative impression of him to simply engage on the topic.

We exchanged contact information so we could talk about strategies and statistics later that night, and a **friendship was born**.

What does this have to do with clicking instantly, likability, and connecting with people?

Well, we lacked any type of click but still managed to be friends... after months of disinterest and disdain.

That was an **outlier** and **exception** to the general rule of meeting new people: **if you don't make a positive first impression, you just won't be friends.** You won't have that opportunity because people won't make an effort towards you or even be open.

Studies have shown that the vast majority of people live and die by **snap judgments** that are made within seconds of meeting someone new. **60** seconds? Try **20**. **10**.

People generally decide where you are on the **spectrum of likability** and whether or not they want to invest more time in you very quickly. It's incredibly **unfair**... but that's the reality of life.

Once that positive or negative impression is set into place, you are every one of your actions is viewed **through it**. If you make it to the **positive** side, you will be given the benefit of the doubt and anything negative will be viewed as circumstantial. Get exiled to the **negative** side, and anything negative will just be further confirmation of your insidious character.

Negative impression? Not even going to bother engaging them ever again. What's the point? There's nothing to gain.

This means that the **snapshot** of yourself that you to others must be compelling... or at least not negative. That's what this book is meant to help you with.

Jason and I got what very few people get in this world – **a second chance**. We were forced to interact so much and so frequently that we were able to overcome any negative first impressions that existed.

That's the importance of the first 60 seconds of any interaction. I very nearly missed out on the best friend that I have, and someone who I have no doubt will be a groomsman at my wedding.

Every other virtue he possessed was overshadowed by a negative *vibe*. It's frightening to think about that applied to ourselves.

In a reality that gives few second chances and even fewer do-overs, what or who could **you** be missing out on if you don't master the art of **clicking instantly**?

1. 60 seconds to everything you want in life.

One of the most important social skills you need to learn is the ability to connect with people instantly.

Most people have busy schedules and don't really have the luxury of time when it comes to personal connections. In social situations, there isn't enough time to truly get a feel for the other person, and to learn to read the other person's signals.

This is why people who are able to connect with others instantly stand out from the crowd. These individuals just go farther in life.

It doesn't matter whether you are selling stuff, trying to meet members of the opposite sex, or just trying to get ahead in your career or business. The ability to connect with people instantly will give you a **competitive advantage**.

People take their first 60 seconds with you and view everything through that **lens**. Every one of your actions after that initial encounter is viewed positively, negatively, or worst of all – not even registered. That means you didn't make an impression at all.

Those first 60 seconds of interaction are crucial, and if you don't learn to make the most of them, you will forever be viewed through a lens of **negativity and skepticism.**

It's a lot like the way a single event can look differently to different people depending on the lens through which they are looking. For example:

Man sends woman flowers. Woman is **smitten** by man, and is therefore flattered and literally swoons when the flower delivery comes.

Man sends woman flowers. Woman is **creeped** out by man, and is therefore distressed by the flowers.

The exact same action, but viewed through a different lens becomes, well... a completely **different action.**

And so it is with your normal everyday interactions. If you've made a great first impression on someone, going forward you'll get the **benefit of the doubt** because your overall character has already been judged to be positive and desirable. If you've made a less than stellar first impression, everything you do after that will only serve to **condemn** you in that person's eyes.

Business benefits.

When you travel for business, you meet a wide variety of individuals in lots of different situations and contexts.

You might be quite uncomfortable in certain situations or certain areas. You might feel far from home and out of your comfort zone, and the sheer unfamiliarity of all these new faces can throw you off.

This is a **natural tendency** for many of us. But, if you can master the art of connecting with people instantly, you will have confidence and even unfamiliar situations will be enjoyable and easy to manage. Connections provide familiarity and a social crutch for the times that we need someone to lean on.

You can take control of your social interactions as long as you send out the **right signals**. This all fits within the ability to make instant connections. Don't think that because you have to make quick connections they have to be contrived, faked or forced. As long as you are **sincere** and are sending out the right signals, you can enjoy a very high comfort level in whatever social context you find yourself in.

This, of course, leads to greater business opportunities. If you focus on honing your skill of connecting with people instantly, you can take advantage of more of these opportunities.

Business is not a meritocracy. The best deals and the best partners aren't always the ones who end up with all of the revenue and business. Business is the epitome of "**it's who you know**" that propels you forward. When you position yourself as likeable, bondable, and relatable, it makes people want to deal with you.

People like **people like themselves** and will almost always prefer to deal with someone who is like them; it gives them that hometown feel of familiarity and comfort.

If you are from an **obscure town in Idaho**, and you run across someone who is also from that town – wouldn't you make an **extra effort** to work with them? It may not even matter if it isn't necessarily the best deal.

So the first 60 seconds are of utmost importance in business simply because it is strong connections and relationships that drive deals to completion.

Social benefits.

There is a lot to be gained from being liked in general. When people like you, they don't normally speak poorly about. In the world of business, or even in dating, selections are often made based on who the "**cleanest**" person is.

When people aren't talking badly about you, you stand out from your competitors; you won't have a **negative reputation**. At the very least, you will be the social hub of a group of people.

This can lead to all sorts of social benefits. You get invited to more parties, which can lead to business opportunities because you will be introduced to more people. This can also lead to greater opportunities as far as the opposite sex is concerned. People will consider you **presentable and likeable**, and will be motivated to introduce you to people they know from the opposite sex.

At the very least, you don't want to be thought of as a

threat, an outsider, or someone who is unwanted.

When you can hit it off instantly with people, your life is going to be a lot easier and better.

Hitting it off with **potential friends**? Well, now you have new friends for shenanigans all around the world.

Hitting it off with the **barista**? Now you're going to get occasional free coffee and preferential treatment.

Hitting it off with the **police officer** that pulled you over (maybe even crying)? You're going to be able to slip out of that ticket worth hundreds of dollars.

Studies have shown that the **number one factor for happiness** in the elderly is how many strong relationships they have. This makes perfect sense: at an advanced age everything except the people in your life and your relationships are ephemeral and temporary.

Of course, this means that connecting instantly with people will just make you a **happier person**.

Romantic benefits.

In our busy day and age, it is very easy and efficient to **weed out and filter** people based on first impressions. In fact, modern dating is like one giant session of speed dating. You only have a **tiny window of time** to make the right impression.

This is especially so with the advent of **online dating**. If something doesn't strike you the right way in the first few moments of a date, another potential date is just a swipe or message away. This has both benefits and drawbacks, and is arguably unhealthy to some degree... but it heavily underscores the importance of those first 60 seconds.

If you don't connect with a certain person instantly, chances are they are gone for good. Chances are because they have a very busy schedule they will dismiss you and move on to the next person. It is very easy for them to get snapped up by somebody else.

We are talking about connecting with people on a meaningful level in 60 seconds or less. This way, you have your foot in the door and everything you do after that works to improve on that great first impression you made.

The first 60 seconds is the **gatekeeper** to the mates you want. It's all part of the **façade**, like your hairstyle, clothes, shoes, and car that combine to form an image that people use to decide whether they want to connect further with you.

Connecting in the first 60 seconds with a potential significant other – that's what we call **romantic chemistry**. Don't underestimate the power of chemistry when it comes to influencing people's decisions about you.

And, just throwing this out there – don't the first 60 seconds heavily influence how we might imagine someone in bed? There's no need to emphasize the importance of this point.

The disadvantages of failing to connect instantly.

When you fail to connect with people instantly, it doesn't necessarily mean that you have made a bad impression.

But you have opened the door to making a bad impression. Increasingly, because people really don't have the luxury of time, we tend to put people into **three buckets**: people that we are sure we like, people we don't know if we like, and people we don't like.

You know you have made a bad impression when you get put in that last bucket. Being put in the middle bucket, however, is not big news. If people are unsure about whether they like you or not, it won't take much for you to eventually be dismissed as somebody who had made a bad impression.

More and more, because people just don't have the time and energy to filter people properly, things are increasingly shaping up to be a **two bucket world**: either you are in the likeable bucket, or in the unlikeable, bad impression bucket.

You have to work harder to change people's impressions of you. In many cases, it can take a long period of time. It can involve many different interactions for you to reverse their initial judgment of your personality or character.

Make no mistake, if you don't hit it off with somebody within the first 60 seconds, chances are they either forget you entirely or they would put you in the disliked bucket. You have to focus on developing the skills that you need to get people to like you instantly.

Without these skills, all the benefits I've listed will just be lost to you. No matter how great your **resume** is, you may get passed over for that job or deal for someone less qualified, but who made a better first impression. No matter how great of a mate you might make, you might get passed over for a bitch or an asshole. You simply don't let the good about you shine out and reach people if you don't make a good impression on them in the first 60 seconds.

Sometimes we hear things like "**I hated him when we first met, but now we're the best of friends!**" We hear about that because it's unusual and stands out. The other, more common situation, meeting someone, not liking them, then avoiding further interaction with them, happens so often it's **not worth mentioning**. Don't be part of that statistic!

The good news is that the art of instant likeability is easier than you think. In many cases, it is purely **modeled behavior**. Just look at how other people are doing it and how they make you feel, and how you can use the same techniques. As long as you are true to yourself, operating from good faith and come from a good place, you will do fine.

2. So what drives instant rapport and connection?

Have you ever noticed that you get along instantly with certain people? What drives that?

In many cases, the connection you feel toward certain people is driven by **random chance or timing**. You can get along with almost anybody if the **context** is right. It also means that if the context isn't right, you will be left out in the cold and feel socially off.

Now, this doesn't mean you can't establish great friendships with these individuals. In many cases, some of the best friendships actually started out on the wrong foot. In many cases, it takes **repeated exposure** or even conscientious design, effort, and coordination to finally get you to warm up to each other. But those close friendships that didn't start out well are the products of luck and repeated opportunities to bond.

Why should we depend on luck or the exactly perfect circumstances to make great impressions and connections? This puts us at the **mercy of our surroundings**, and even begins to build a sort of mental dependency on having the correct ingredients. Naturally, this can prevent action any time the right mixture isn't present, and can be more of a crutch than a help, so it's important to realize that you don't need luck to make a great impression.

Instant connections by design.

This book will help you establish **rapport through purposeful design**. I will teach you ways to intentionally create situations that can lead to better rapport. I will walk you through the mindsets you need to adopt that will open you up to instant, personal connections.

I focus on a designed, purposeful approach to rapport and connection because relying on random chance and organic situations for instant connection can lead nowhere. In fact, you could wait forever to make friends this way. You have to understand that random chance and organic connections happen because of luck. That's what makes them random.

You, and the people you are trying to connect with, just find yourself in a particular setting and situation that triggers certain mindsets allowing you to connect with each other. If you are expecting things to line up so that you can make friends in this more organic and "natural" way, you will probably be waiting a long time depending on your schedule, your lifestyle, or the country you're from.

It might be inconvenient, if not outright impossible, to rely on random chance to have an **organic rapport** take place. You need to take matters into your own hands. You need to be systematic and methodical in establishing rapport and connection. Otherwise, you might miss the boat on what could otherwise be a great friendship.

Humans and likability?

Human beings are **social creatures**. We are genetically programmed to work with, and in, groups. That's just part of who we are. And since social interaction is hardwired into our natural constitution and survival, it is crucial that we find ourselves wanting others to like us.

Many people seem to have grown past this stage and don't feel an overbearing need to be liked, but our inherent tendency is still there. Knowing this gives you a crucial tool needed to reach out to other people.

If you feel a need to be liked, guess what? Other people feel that need too. By allowing yourself to make the first move, you can get other people to like you in return. You are all operating from the same place. You all have a need to be liked, and the price that you are willing to pay to be liked is to like others in return.

What can people gain from being in social groups or avoiding isolation?

It is very hard to shake off thousands of years of psychological evolution. You have to remember that people who were solitary or reclusive thousands, if not millions, of years ago probably did not pass on their genes. Considering how harsh the landscape was back then, hanging out in social groups was a matter of **life and death**.

A lot of our need to be accepted, and our need to reach out to others was passed along in humanity's gene pool. This is why even the most reclusive person still has the capacity to feel the need to belong. Even in our modern age, with all of our **technology and economic** improvements, there are still solid gains to be made by being part of a social group.

First, you are able to work your connections to obtain better paying jobs, establish better income opportunities, and meet members of the opposite sex that come from the same social circles as you. Study after study show that people tend to look for individuals who share their values. Put simply, they are looking for people who have their same social level or at least the values of that social level. You can try to find those people randomly, but you will have a hard time taking that approach. You can use your social networks, and this is where being a social person, or hanging out in social networks, can pay off.

<u>Try this exercise.</u>

Everybody has the ability to connect. Don't think you are so completely socially awkward that you have lost this ability. As I mentioned earlier, our ancestors needed to be social because they needed it to survive. They needed to hang out in packs so they could hunt and live another day.

This pack mentality survives in our genes to this very day. Even if you consider yourself highly socially reclusive and anti-social, you still have elements of that ability.

When was the last time a new person came into your group of friends? How were they accepted and why? Did they initially bond with one person in the group who then vouched for them?

Think about what they did to make a favorable impression on you, and pay close attention the next time someone new is introduced to your group of friends.

What kind of feeling did you get? Did you notice how people send signals to each other to make them feel welcome? They ask them about what they've been doing. They share stuff about the places they've been to, the new dishes they've eaten and new adventures they've been on. They also share news and gossip.

It all serves a greater purpose – there is a relaxed and calming atmosphere created that allows you to open up to new people. When they open up to you, you open up to them, and you feel that you belong.

This is the bond that any social group regularly practices. If you stand back and analyze what is going on, you can identify certain triggers. The best news is that you can work those triggers so that you can bond with complete strangers in 60 seconds or less.

3. Best attitudes and practices to connect instantly.

Your ability to connect with people is a reflection of your attitude. If you think new people or social situations are scary, guess what? Chances are you are not going to connect that well with unfamiliar people.

The key lesson you need to wrap your mind around is that **your mental perception dictates your external reality**. What you perceive the world and others to be will turn out to be the reality. The truth that we all need to understand is that we each have our own pair of lens when it comes to perceiving reality and the truth. Everything that we sense is filtered through these lens.

If you see through **lens** that are very negative and fearful, chances are that your life will not be as pleasant as you would like. You will think that the world is hostile and not really a place of easy friendships and good times.

On the other hand, if you choose a different pair of **lens**, ones that make you very curious and interested in how other people live, where they are from, and what it is like to be with them, you will get very different results.

You will notice that people like hanging out with you. You will find that you get invited to more parties. Life in general will be more fun or, at the very least, more tolerable. It's your choice.

Everybody has this pair of lens. Unfortunately, most of us are unaware that we are even wearing these lens. A key part of this mindset is, of course, our attitude. There are different parts to this mindset. This mindset is composed of mental framework, philosophies, values, assumptions and expectations. **But the biggest part is attitude.**

Great attitudes for easier connections.

If you want to connect with people faster, more efficiently and more effectively, you only need to adopt the right attitude.

In fact, even if you don't feel that you have this attitude at first, you can start acting like you have it. Eventually, the signals that people give you will start reinforcing that attitude.

What is the right attitude when it comes to establishing quick rapport and personal connection with somebody new?

Think along these lines: **I wonder what *they* are like. What can they teach me? What do we have in common? What are they great at and what can they teach me?** Ask yourself these questions. When you meet new people, feel the positive emotions that they carry. Make it your mission to find out everything you possibly can about them.

When you think about these attitudes, there's no reason to think they aren't true. We're not always the best at everything we try our hand at, and we're not all that and a bag of chips. Other people have at least five things that they can teach us about in a pinch – make it your mission and attitude to find those things and gain value from others, as well **as impart your own**.

Even if you are feeling apprehensive, insecure, have low self-esteem or low self-confidence, block out those negative signals and just let the questions carry you. By fostering a **genuine sense of curiosity** and adventure to push you forward, you can connect easily and quickly with people. This is all part of a good social attitude.

If you don't actually think that other people are interesting or can provide you anything of value (be it just information or entertainment), then you are likely to act that way and not establish any sort of connection.

Bad social attitudes to avoid.

While I phrase the good attitude you should have when it comes to social connections in terms of **questions**, when it comes to a poor social attitude, I'm going to describe it in terms of **situations**. If you find yourself in these situations, you have a bad or poor attitude when it comes to establishing rapport and connections.

If you go into any kind of social situation with a **specific goal**, chances are things are not going to pan out. Chances are you will project a poor attitude. Your goals put pressure on you to be social. When you are feeling pressured, it is easier to mess up. It also gives you blinders.

Yes, focus is sometimes good, but it can also make you oblivious to potential pathways for connection while in pursuit of that goal. In other words, because you're too focused on X, you miss the opportunities for Y and Z, opportunities that might have been extremely fruitful on their own.

Another situation that can lead to a poor social attitude is going in with **expectations**. If you expect to make a bunch of quick connections, chances are things will not turn out right. Instead of seeming excited and welcoming, you will come off as brusque, insensitive, or calculated and scheming.

This will also seep into the air that you project in your social situation – people with expectations act as if they deserve things, and as if they don't have to work as hard for them. People are more astute than you might think, and people will catch on to this attitude that you emanate.

Finally, one of the worst attitudes you can adopt is to go into any kind of social situation thinking that the **people there are not worth your time**. People easily pick up on this. People can quickly detect if you feel that they are beneath you. I mentioned earlier that literally everyone has worth to you, even though it may not seem like it initially.

You're also not a combination of Beyonce and Maroon 5, so why would you ever feel that you are better than others? If you feel that way, then that should be additional motivation to dig deeper and find out the interesting traits that others possess underneath the surface. Everyone is worth your time, and no one is inherently beneath you.

Best practices.

It is very easy to hit it off quickly with a random stranger. You just need to do one thing: **give them your full attention**. When you are in front of them, with neutral body language signs, give them your full attention, listen to them, look them straight in the eye, and essentially send out signals that you are welcoming and open to them; they will open up to you.

People are not stones that have no emotional resonance. We are always involved in a call-and-response relationship with whoever is in front of us. When you send off the right signals and give that person your full attention, that person will send signals back. This can lead to an upward spiral or it can lead to a downward spiral.

Try this exercise.

The next time you go out to a cafe or to a store, focus on working on your ability to establish quick rapport. You can do this by working with a member of a **captive audience**. I am, of course, talking about people who work at the cafe or store. The Starbucks **barista** or the store **cashier** doesn't have any place to go. That's their job. They are supposed to interact with you.

And the best part is they are required to be nice to you. So even if you fall flat on your face trying to make a quick personal connection, it won't matter because you will not feel the sting of rejection or mockery because these people are paid to be nice to you. Once you are in front of one of them, and they have the space and time to entertain you, ask them how they are. Ask them how their day is going.

They will give you certain answers. Be quick to pick up on certain answers that you can expand on. By giving them your full attention and focusing your conversation on them, you will be surprised how well you will hit it off. You have to remember that people love to talk about themselves. When you give people a forum to talk about themselves, they will take that opportunity. This establishes a great personal rapport and connection.

What happens if you screw up and the conversation goes nowhere? Nothing. And that's the best part. These people are paid to be nice to you. You can try again tomorrow, and the day after, and the day after that - until you succeed.

Above all else, imagine what the barista or cashier can **teach you**!

4. What first impression are you sending out?

Connecting with people in 60 seconds is all about **first impressions**. You might think that 60 seconds is too short a time to get a working, or even practical, impression of someone. You would be completely wrong.

In fact, if you ever use the **Internet**, you make **snap judgments** all the time.

How many search results have you gotten from Google when you click on a link and almost immediately bounce back to the search results you were looking at? I would venture to say that you do this regularly. This is how most people navigate the Internet... and that's how we navigate our **real world social circles** as well.

Depending on your job, the social circles you hang out in, or your particular lifestyle, you are going to meet a lot of different people. Obviously, we don't make instant connections and deep friendships with the **vast majority** of these people. There are just so many people whom we interact with on a day to day basis. Instead, we make snap judgments for our **sanity** and for the sake of **efficiency**.

These judgments take place in 60 seconds or less. In fact, most of them take place in just a few seconds. It doesn't take much to read people. This is the secret that you need to understand when it comes to connecting instantly with people.

People read into each other all the time. You have to be aware of this process and control it so that it works to your favor. If you only rely on random chance and luck to make a great first impression, you will be waiting for a long time.

As I mentioned earlier, organic and unplanned great first impressions rarely take place. Why? They require certain special circumstances and situations to be in play for them to pan out. If those are not happening, you are not going to make the best impression.

Does this mean that everything is lost? **Absolutely not**.

You can come back again and try to make a better impression next time. But it takes much more work, and probably more time to reverse the first impression you made. You have to go into any kind of social situation where you are meeting new people with the right toolkit. You have to have the right strategy in place.

You wouldn't be reading this book if your normal method worked wonderfully for you, right? Keep the following factors in mind when trying to craft a great first impression, so you can make instant friends.

<u>Be aware of the verbal signals you are sending out.</u>

When you are saying hello to people, did you know that you are already sending out a message? The message is not so much what you say, but how you say it.

Saying "Hello" to somebody in can be received in many different ways depending on your **tone of voice**. If you say it in a flat tone, chances are that the other person will respond coldly and in a very business-like manner. But if you say, "Hello!" in a friendly, open and, most important, excited way, they can't help but respond favorably.

You have to remember that just because you greet people excitedly and with a lot of eagerness and emotion, it doesn't necessarily mean they will bounce back those signals to you. Some people are just naturally **reserved**. Some people seem naturally **cold**. You need to look at the overall context of how they receive you.

For example, if you say hello in an excited way to somebody who is very reserved, they will probably say hello back, but with a smile. To them, it means that you are in a positive space with them. **That's all you should expect**. This person is reserved, so you shouldn't expect that person to be as physically excited as you.

Once that friendship matures and goes deeper, then they will allow themselves to show a little bit more excitement. Just because they might not express overtly doesn't mean they aren't looking for it from you and from other people.

Regardless, look for signs of positivity. Different people show positivity in different ways. We are all different emotional creatures and we have different emotional levels. Deal with it. What's important is to detect a positive response and contrast that with negative or cold response.

Be clear about the non-verbal signals you are sending out.

Besides the words coming out of your mouth, you are also sending out **non-verbal signals**. This is important. You have to make sure that what's going on with your face is sending out the right kind of message and the message you mean to be sending.

There are many professionals, people and politicians who have perpetual smiles on their faces. It's like a **clown mask**. They are constantly happy and positive. That doesn't fool anyone, and it can actually be a negative thing. We frequently call these people **fake**, don't we?

If you have a generic smile on your face that you give to everybody you meet, you are not going to make much of a positive impression. People will be neutral to you at the very best. The reason for this is that people like to be received on a **personal level**.

At the very least, give them their own personal smiles. Customize your engagement with them in terms of your facial expressions and mannerism so that they feel that you are actually engaging them on a one-to-one level. Don't give them that same generic smile that you give everybody else. On a practical level, this means that when you react to what someone is saying, have a blank expression on your face for a split second before bursting into a smile – this gives the impression that the smile is clearly for, and caused by them.

Another set of non-verbal signals you need to be keenly aware of is your **body language signals.** Don't cross your arms. Don't cross your legs. Be open. At the very least, use neutral body language signals. Make sure you are facing them completely. Make sure you are looking at them in the eye, and you are nodding your head or giving off some signals that you are actually listening to them. People like to be the center of the show.

If, however, it is obvious that you don't really care about what they have to say, that will kill your personal connection. If you want people to be interested in you, make sure you are interested in them first. At the very least, give a convincing set of verbal and non- verbal signals to communicate your **level of engagement**.

Try this exercise.

Ask five of your friends to reach back into their memory banks and tell you a story about their **first impression of you**. But tell them to give it to you in the form of one word adjectives. You will probably get a long list of adjectives.

Some of your friends might say that you are exciting. Others will say you are intelligent. Even others might say that you are introspective and deep. Regardless, you need to come up with a long list of adjectives.

You should not be offended or take hold it against them if somebody's adjectives are negative. We are all human beings. We are all works in progress. None of us are perfect. Expect a list of positive adjectives and a list of **not-so-positive** adjectives.

After you've gotten the list from your friends, go in front of a mirror and practice facial expressions, tones of voice, and greetings or sayings that **mirror these adjectives**. Exaggerate them.

If a friend of yours said that you were intelligent, look at yourself in the mirror and act in a way that an intelligent interesting person would. If somebody said that you were dreamy and idealistic, look in the mirror and figure out what kind of mannerisms or gestures a dreamy or idealistic person would project.

The whole point of this exercise is to be aware of the non-verbal and verbal signals that you are sending out, so you can fine-tune them. You need to do this for both positive and negative adjectives that you get. By being aware of the signals you are sending out, you are well on the road to controlling those signals later on.

You can also learn the ways that you can appear like those positive adjectives by practicing them.

5. Inbound and outbound positivity.

The next time you find yourself among a group of people, you will notice that there is at least one person that everybody tends to **gravitate** toward.

There's just something about that one person in the group that attracts attention and gains a lot of respect and good feelings. Look for it in your own circle of friends and the groups of people around you.

The reason one person tends to become the center of attention is because that person radiates positivity. That person makes people **feel good** about themselves. That person contributes something to the atmosphere that makes people feel welcomed, appreciated, and good about themselves. It's no surprise that people want to be around people like this.

They're not the life of the party, and they're not the most charming people, but there is just something that makes people want to be around them. At our core, we are mere animals that occasionally succumb to **positive conditioning**. If someone makes us feel good, shows interest in us, and compliments us, we want to be around them! Some people can do this with baked goods, others can do this with their positivity.

You can do it too. There is no mystery to becoming a person that is instantly likeable within an open social setting. Here are some tips on how to radiate positivity for instant likeability.

Be quick to praise.

As long as you are eager and sincere, your praises are always welcome. You might think it would be hard to praise somebody you've just met. In fact, it's easier than you think.

All of us have positive and negative aspects. Unfortunately, we tend to focus too much on the negative sides of our beings, and we don't spend enough time looking at our positive sides. Everybody has a positive side, even if it's purely superficial like our appearance, our hair, our teeth, or our skin. There is something positive about **everybody**.

Focus on that most positive superficial side to a person and sincerely compliment them about it. Praise them.

What happens when you do this is that you trigger one of the most fundamental weaknesses humans have: we are all starved for **attention**. We are all starved for **compliments**. We like to be put in the spotlight and given the attention that we feel we deserve. When you zero in on one part of a person that is obvious to others, like their physical appearance, their hair, their outfit, or whatever factor that is easily observable, you give them the attention that they crave deep down.

As long as you are sincere, things will go over well. You don't want to go over the top. You don't want to overplay your hand so that it looks as if you're mocking the person. You have to remember that there is a thin line between sincere praise, flattery, and outright mockery and insult. You have to know where that line is so you don't go over it.

Give people the credit they deserve, or that you know that they **crave**. This shows a deep understanding of their **motivations**, and they will feel closer to you immediately for sharing the same train of thought and being on the same wavelength. It can be as simple as sharing a knowing glance and nod about something.

<u>Freely compliment people.</u>

Now, you might be thinking, "Well, what's the big difference between praising and complimenting people? Aren't they the same?" Well, for the most part, they are very similar but there is one key point of distinction.

When you praise somebody, you are praising the person for making a good decision or praising some sort of action or some sort of character trait about that person. You're praising the person's character. You're presenting the person's character or personal value in a positive light.

When you compliment, you're more **superficial**. You look at what they've done or what they are wearing, and you're just focused on that. This is a small distinction, but it can mean a lot.

When you compliment, you have a lot more **leeway** when it comes to your positivity. It's harder for you to go over the top and come off as if you're mocking the person. Still, you need to watch your words because you want to open a gateway of positivity so you can bond with that person. You don't want to cross the line and come off as if you are insincere or are mocking the person.

People aren't really complimented that much on a daily basis – **especially men**. We can easily see this because most people don't know how to take a true and genuine compliment without a bit of awkward fumbling. Make it a goal to see people fumble about the compliments you give them – that means it impacts them more because they simply don't get many – and it impacts your relationship more.

Validate people.

Another key aspect of radiating positivity is when you validate people. Validation goes beyond praising and complimenting. Validation, above all else, is about making people feel good about what they feel.

When you make people feel good, people eventually identify you with that good feeling. Since most people are drawn to pleasure and tend to run away from pain, they will be drawn to you. You make them feel good, at ease, and comfortable. Not surprisingly, they want to have you around more of the time.

So relate with people. **Make them feel heard**. Listen to their rants, whether happy or sad. Agree with them and know that they have someone in their corner.

Laugh at their jokes.

Humor is very **personal**. What you find funny and what makes you laugh might not the same for someone else. A lot of your personality is wrapped up in what you find humorous.

This is why it's really important that you laugh at somebody's joke. It may be a forced or fake laugh, but the message it sends is important. It shows that you've heard the other person, that you are paying attention and that you've understood them. By laughing with them, you've let them know you appreciate them, and that you like them.

People like to be accepted. People like to feel that they belong somewhere. When you make someone feel those things, you send a powerful subconscious signal to them that they should hang around with you more often.

When you laugh at people's jokes, you make them feel validated and like a funny person. Many people self-identify as a funny or humorous person, so this gives them a stronger sense of self-worth because you've confirmed their humor. If you tried to demonstrate something that you felt was core to your being, and people disagreed, how would that make you feel? Some variation of the word "**identity crisis**" would probably be in order.

Radiating positivity is not fake or manipulative.

As long as you are sincere and as long as your intentions are good, radiating positivity is not fraudulent. You have to remember that the world can be a negative and hostile place. When you are the only person who tends to look at the positive or bright side of things consistently, people will be drawn to you. You become a beacon of light and hope to them and at the same time, they make you feel good about yourself. There's nothing wrong with this situation as long as you are clear about your intentions and your intentions are good.

Is this lying? Depends how you view **society**. If you believe that society should be a cauldron of brutal honesty and truth… well, you're just not living in **reality**.

Is it **patronizing**? No. you aren't purporting to actually feel these emotions, but rather just demonstrate them outwardly to achieve your goal of getting closer to people. Saying that you feel an emotion when you don't is patronizing, but ackn**owledging someone's actions or words in a positive sense is simply a powerful social cue** -- and it's also courteous.

Try this exercise.

Think of at least five people you've talked to in the past day. Come up with a mental picture of each one. Try to identify positive things about them. Now, try to verbalize those positive things in the form of compliments.

Edit yourself so that the compliments are short, to the point, and very clear. Keep editing until you can verbalize these compliments in a very powerful and clear way. Think about whether they **identify** with them, or if the compliment is about a core part of their identity. This is how you set yourself up for complimenting these people effectively the next time you meet them.

6. Zero effort, small acts of service endear people to you.

According to popular wisdom, there are **five love languages**. These are the ways we communicate affection and love to special people in our lives.

The first is to simply **say it**. This is the verbal language. If you love somebody, tell them you love them. If you are a verbal person, you like people you care about to tell you that they love you. This verbal declaration reaffirms you and makes you feel good about yourself. Similarly, this is how you express your love and affection to others.

The second way is **physical touch**. Some people aren't as responsive to being told they are appreciated or loved, but they like a reassuring touch. This type of person likes to be touched and loves to touch in return.

The third way is to **give gifts**. Some people measure emotional commitment by the number of gifts they receive. Of course, this person also reciprocates emotional bonding by giving gifts in return.

It's very easy to think that this type of person is materialistic, but that would be missing the point entirely.

Gift-givers don't focus on the value of the gift. Instead, they focus on the thought behind the gift. They think that the ability to give of yourself in the form of a gift is the highest form of emotional communication. It's not the amount you paid for the item you're giving. It's more about the thought, the care, the preparation, and the bother you went through to get the gift in the first place.

The fourth way to show somebody you care about them is to simply spend **quality time** with them. We're not talking about just being in the same room with them. That's just time spent together and really doesn't matter all that much if your attention is focused somewhere else.

People who respond to this fourth way are looking for quality time. Quality time is when your attention is focused on the needs of the other person. You may not be solving another person's problems, but as long as you are occupying the same space and focused intently on what they have to say, or just enjoying your time with them, that is good enough.

Keep in mind that with quality time, what is important is quality, not quantity. As mentioned above, you can spend tons of time in the same room, but if you're not really communicating and if you're not really radiating positivity to each other, you're not spending quality time.

Finally, the fifth way is to perform **small acts of service**. For example, you may sweep somebody's floor, help them with the dishes, and help them with stuff at work. Regardless of what you do, these small acts of going beyond yourself and taking care of the needs of somebody else mean a lot to them. It shows them that you actually care.

If you want to instantly connect with people, and you want people to like you instantly, you might want to do a lot of **small acts of service** for them. In fact, this particular love language applies to most people, and can apply **out of the sphere of relationships**. The other love languages apply, but in varying degrees outside of your significant other because you can't just go around instigating heavy touch principles at a networking event.

So this one is the one that we can utilize the most in everyday situations, and once you think about it, you'll see that you can indeed implement it easily into your life.

You have to remember that anybody can say they support you, but if you can't see the support in terms of their actions, their words are meaningless to you. It's the small acts that really bring home the point that this person is in it with you and can go all the way. Small acts of service **engender loyalty**.

It shows thoughtfulness.

When somebody goes out of their way to do all these things for you, it shows that they think about you. At the very least, it shows that you are a **priority** to them. This means a lot, and people will make many positive inferences about your relationship.

At the very least, they will feel that they are something of a priority to you, and they will reciprocate accordingly and make you a higher priority than you were before.

<u>People become indebted to you.</u>

When you do small acts of service that really don't take much effort on your part, or cost you much money, you might think that the small act isn't really worth much. You'd be surprised.

People pay in two ways: they either pay in **money** or in **emotional debt**. When they see an act of service, they pay in terms of emotional debt. They will see that you made an effort, and you went an **extra mile**. When they feel this way, their debt of gratitude to you builds up over time. Eventually, they will think more favorably of you when they compare you to their other friends who simply just give them lip service or pat them on the back or give them warm hugs. At the end of the day, it's your actual act of service and going out of your way that makes you stand apart from everybody else. This makes you instantly likeable, and this cements that personal bond.

If it's not an emotional debt, then they literally will pay you back in the same way by doing something for you. This is **relationship building** at its finest.

This means that you have nothing to lose. You'll either get back the investment you put in... or you'll find someone emotionally indebted to you, the value of which is frankly incalculable.

<u>Just remember not to ask for anything in return.</u>

I saved the most important part for last. Doing small acts of service helps you become more likeable. Small acts of service pave the way for a long and deep friendship.

However, don't spoil everything by doing things with the intention of asking for something in return. When you do that, you're not doing acts of service, you're actually working, you're **manipulating** people, and you're essentially trying to do a **business deal**.

What you're trying to do with small acts of service is to get people to like you, and a key component of that is **selflessness**. The world is full of selfish people, and it really is refreshing to see somebody who will go out of their way to help someone else with one small act of service. Don't spoil it by asking for something in return.

You might have your ulterior motives, and you might be calculating in the tasks that you perform, but let the tasks speak for themselves. Once you ask for something in return for a small act that you've done for someone else, you risk that person thinking, "Oh, *that's* why he did that for me ..." You are effectively labeled as manipulative.

But if you're doing something with the hidden motive of trying to get something from someone else, then perhaps manipulative is actually the proper term.

Try this exercise.

Next time you're outside of your home, say at a café or restaurant, look around at the other people there. How would you be able to **improve or enrich** their lives? What would you be able to do for them?

It can be something as small as grabbing them a napkin without them asking, or making sure that their chair is clean. The more you practice this way of thinking, the more you will be able to identify small ways and acts of service that you can use on a **daily basis** to make people appreciate and like you more. It's not easy to start with, but it just takes a little bit of practice to see that you can always enrich people's lives – at little or no cost to yourself.

7. People bond through their imperfections; perfection is uncomfortable.

A common misconception regarding instant likeability is that we have to be everything to **everybody** that we meet. I hope you can already see what's wrong with this concept.

Just as it's impossible to please all the people all of the time, it really is a waste of time to be **100% safe** so you can be likeable. You have to remember that when you try to play it safe, you are possibly **downplaying**, or even denying, a lot of the things about you that could make you so likeable. You have to get rid of the idea of perfection or '100% safe personality.' No such animal exists. Regardless of how safe you play things, someone somehow someway somewhere will feel you rubbed them the wrong way.

In another way, this is simply playing to **NOT LOSE**. When you do this you turn yourself into a **cup of chicken broth** – chicken broth goes with everything but doesn't particularly have any inherent flavor of its own. It needs other ingredients to shine. Is this you? Is this what you want to be?

By playing it safe 100% of the time, you will also have a

difficult time finding true friends. True friends aren't interested in a vanilla version of you, so the only people that you are attracting when you are vanilla-safe are people that might not embrace the real you. **What's the point of that?**

Playing it safe makes you the type of person that your true friends probably wouldn't be attracted to.

So ditch playing it safe and project yourself.

Embrace your flaws – no one else will do it for you

We are all imperfect, and that's what makes us likeable. It's not so much how you conform to an ideal that makes people like and admire you. Instead, it's your **quirks**, your **imperfections**, and your **rough spots** that make you endearing. These are what make you a real person. We are all works in progress. This is relatable because everyone else has rough spots, and everyone else has flaws. We are all working toward something, and it's easier to connect to someone that you feel has so much in common with you; you are both on the same journey.

While we do have our ideals, we tend to look at each other and size each other up by our imperfections. We are drawn to people that are imperfect. While we respect people that seem perfect, we really don't feel we have much in common with them. As a result, when you try to be perfect, you easily become forgettable.

Your imperfections make people relaxed.

When you're not 100% safe, meaning your imperfections are visible, it makes others relaxed. It sets them at ease with the fact that you're a human being just like them. Just as a junior high school class will be more at ease with a **substitute teacher** who swears from time to time, when you let other people see your rough spots, it lets other people relax.

When you're comfortable with your flaws, other people will be too. This is easily illustrated through the opposite – when you're **NOT comfortable** with your flaws, people will be uneasy as well. If you are obese and highly defensive about your weight and anything to do with food or diet... imagine how uncomfortable people will be about it? They will know that it's a huge point of contention with you and be sure to avoid those things when they are around you ... or just avoid you in general.

But if you are at ease with being a little overweight, and can maybe even poke fun of yourself, it puts other people at ease. They know they don't have to **walk on eggshells** around you. Having to restrict everything you say is a terrible and limiting feeling and people don't like it.

People highly dislike perfection. It creeps them out, and worst of all, brings out the insecurities that we all have. It makes them self-conscious and shine a light into themselves when they see something that they feel they want to achieve but can't. It's a bummer of a feeling. That's why celebrities are sometimes encouraged to show some vulnerability and flaws. It allows us to relate to them and makes them more human and ultimately more likeable.

<u>Why playing it safe doesn't work.</u>

The thing about social interaction is that people are very **conservative**. They're always afraid they will say the wrong thing, make the wrong move, and basically ruin whatever bond they have with other people. At the very least, they don't want to make the wrong impression.

Well, if you're operating in an atmosphere where people are tip toeing around on eggshells in order not offend other people, there is a climate of fear. There is a forbidding atmosphere. People may be respectful and polite, but that doesn't result in instant likeability. This type of environment doesn't lead to people opening up quickly to each other, which is the only way to develop deep personal bonds.

Instead, people are more open to others who strike them as a little bit off. These are people who are weird, who show their inappropriate side, who are a bit on the margins, and who are edgy. Why are these people so much more interesting than "safe" people? They stand out! They are easier to notice.

Now, think hard: can you remember somebody who is "safe" and who is utterly conventional? Chances are you probably **can't**. Why? Because they **melt into the background**. They completely blend into the woodwork, and they are boring and forgettable.

Repeat after me: if you are safe, you are boring and forgettable.

What's the worst that can happen? The worst that can

happen is you won't see these people again. What's the best that can happen? They identify with your rough spot, your unpolished side, your idiosyncrasies, and you connect. In some cases, you might even develop a lifelong friend... at least you give yourself the opportunity by not playing it safe.

Don't start off inappropriate but don't be afraid to go there either.

Don't be so afraid of seeming **offensive or tasteless** that you make all your conversations boring and "safe."

Put another way, don't shy away from **off color subjects**. Vulgarity and nasty topics will come up. We can't control where a conversation goes. Just let others take the lead regarding "off" topics – and when they do, don't be afraid to follow their lead and explore them.

Don't dwell on them, but don't evade them either. Inappropriate topics often provide the most laughs out of any conversation, and there's another powerful psychological effect when you delve into these intimate and personal issues: **only good friends** talk to each other about inappropriate situations when their guards are down. Just another way you can disguise yourself as, and become, a good friend in record time.

Try this exercise.

Write out a list of ten **taboo or "offensive" or vulgar topics**. Think of how these can come up in a conversation. Map out how the conversation can proceed when these topics come up. In front of a mirror, watch yourself raise these issues one by one and look at your facial expression and bearing when you raise them. Pay attention to your tone of voice. How well do you play these awkward topics? What are the chances of their killing the conversation?

Figure out how to control the flow of the conversation so the talk can lead to other topics and extend the discussion. Figure out how to manage the flow of the conversation so you come off as an interesting hero rather than a tacky awkward conversation-killing boor. Keep practicing until you get the signals right.

Next, raise these topics with a friend.

Track their reaction. What can you say to regain control of the conversation? What kind of presentation or set of signals do you send that leads them to feel closer to you. Keep in mind that taboo topics aren't always conversation killers and don't need to be awkward. If anything, they often lead to **"you too?!"** moments that draw friends closer or create instant bonds between two people who are otherwise strangers. In everything you do, try to avoid playing it safe. When you play things safe, you are easily forgotten.

8. Open and friendly body language is as important as your words.

You can say whatever you want, but the words from your mouth are often overshadowed by your **body language**. You have to remember that people are always reading you, even if unconsciously. The worst part of it is that your words are only part of the equation. In fact, you don't even have to say anything. Your actions can definitely speak louder than your words.

You have to be very careful regarding the signals you send out based on how you stand, how you handle your arms, how you present your chest, how you look at people, and other physical signals. Add to this mix the tone of voice you use and your facial expressions. All these add together to paint a picture that people perceive on an emotional level.

This is what makes the body language such a great thing and such a terrifying thing at the same time. If you are unaware or are totally clueless regarding your body language and overall impression you are creating, you will be completely left in the dark about why you are able to make instant connections, or why you are having a tough time connecting to people on a personal level.

<u>Your body language determines your approachability.</u>

People are always afraid of rejection. I don't care how well adjusted you are, or how good you are with people.

Not surprisingly, we tend to do a **quick scan** of other people before we approach them. We only want to approach people that we are sure won't reject us. We want to approach people that we think have a high likelihood of giving us the emotional payoff that we are looking for. At a minimum, we want to avoid people that might dismiss us or make us feel ill at ease; people who might outright reject us or make us feel unwelcome. We're looking for people who are **agreeable and approachable**.

The problem is you might be displaying the kinds of body language signals that tell people that you shouldn't be approached. Alternately, you might be sending out signals that you will judge somebody or make them feel unwelcome or beneath you for approaching you. So be very careful about what you do with your body and how you present yourself. You don't even have to say a word.

<u>Make sure your body language is always consistent with your words.</u>

A very common way to put off people is when the words coming out of your mouth are in stark **contrast** with the signals you're sending out with your gestures, mannerisms, and overall body language. You're saying one thing, but you're actually doing another.

When people receive **inconsistent signals**, they usually do one of two things: either they back off, or they get confused. Neither of these situations is good or work for you to foster deep and lasting personal bonds. They certainly don't make you look friendly and open. They put you in a gray area where people don't know how to treat you. This is not exactly where you want to be. You want people to feel good around you and feel at ease.

It's always a good idea to make sure that whatever words you're saying are consistent with your body language signals. If you are speaking words of friendliness and positivity, make sure that you have a smile, your **tone of voice** is light and eager, your **chest** is open, and you don't cross your **arms**. Always make sure that these other signals that you normally send out are positive. Or, at the very least, make sure that they are neutral and don't contradict the verbal messages that you are sending out.

Try this exercise.

Stand in front of a mirror and pretend you're meeting new people. Pay attention to two things. First, pay attention to your greeting and what you're saying. Next, pay attention to your facial expression, your posture, how your arms are positioned, how your chest is positioned, and how you make eye contact. Do you see any **discrepancies**? Do you see any **inconsistencies**?

Make sure that how you look in the mirror reflects the kind of impression you want to make in the minds of the people that you're meeting. Once you've reached that consistency, then you can go out into the real world and try this out.

Basic body language tips for openness and friendliness.

Always make sure that you are facing somebody completely. Don't turn your body. Don't lean back or lean to the side. Above all else, make sure that your feet are not facing toward the door or somewhere else. Make it clear to them that they have your **full attention**. It communicates to them that they are important to you, and that you want to spend time with them.

However, if your feet are facing away or your body is oriented in some **other direction**, it communicates that you're not really interested in what they have to say. You don't really care about dealing with them. Of course, your words may lead somebody to conclude otherwise, but actions speak louder than words.

Try not to **fidget**. When you fidget, like playing with your thumbs, or playing air piano on your desk, it gives the impression that you don't want to be there, and that you would rather be doing something else. Again, this doesn't make people feel treasured, appreciated, or liked, and if they don't feel appreciated or liked, they will reflect that same sentiment back at you.

Try this body language exercise.

Watch yourself in the mirror and watch your arms as you talk. What kind of impression does your arm position give you when you talk? Is it positive or negative? Open or closed? Tensed or relaxed? Welcoming or standoffish? If negative, can you change your arm position to ensure that it sends out the right signals?

Keep experimenting until you feel that the way you move your arms or the way you position your arms sends out a positive and welcoming message. Do the same for your posture and your facial expressions. Keep experimenting until your expressions and mannerisms trigger feelings of openness and friendliness.

9. Prepare to connect with rehearsed stories.

As I've mentioned, expecting to hit it off well with somebody on a purely organic or random basis is impractical.

Everything has to be lined up properly for you to hit it off with somebody in a purely natural and unscripted manner. This whole book is all about you taking steps so you can make that situation happen on a fairly predictable basis. **Chemistry and *clicking*** can be planned – that's why we're improving our social skills.

One of the best ways you can prepare to make a great first impression is to come up with **prepared stories** for the questions that you know you'll run into on a daily basis.

People love stories. Stories are how people navigate the world, and relate to each other. If you break it down, most great conversations are **exchanges of interrelated stories** that build upon each other.

Our memory banks are exposed to countless potential entries a day and clearly not all of them make it. In fact, we only embed a tiny fraction in our consciousness - we filter the rest out.

By and large, the things we do remember aren't always a choice, but we remember them because they have an **emotional element** to them. We relate to them, they make us feel, or otherwise affect us in an emotional way with respect to our personal narrative and identity.

Stories are likable and relatable.

Stories help you become more likable because you instantly get into people's minds. When you tell a story, you immediately relate to the other person based on the content of your story. Most of all, it's the quickest way to find a way to actually connect with a new person.

How many times a day are you asked **how your weekend was**? These are **softball** questions that you can knock out of the park if you prepare stories for them to instantly connect and make a great impression on people.

How was your weekend?

Oh, y'know, same old. You?

This is great – if you want to be forgettable and not make an impression. This is such a simple step that most people miss, but you can start taking advantage of today.

Funny stories.

When you have a funny story, you entertain people around

you.

This sounds obvious, but it is important because **entertainment** is one of the main reasons people engage in conversation.

It's also important because people won't consider you threatening, hostile, or off-putting. Of course, that's the opposite of a positive first impression, but it also means that people will open up to you much more easily. They will accept the stories you share at face value, without questioning the information or your character. Trust can start here, and it can lead to an exchange of stories.

Relatable stories.

Relatability is actually more important than the humor of a story. The reason is simple. If you can **bond** over something you have in common with someone else, even if it's relatively shallow, then you have unlocked any gates they may have put up in front of you.

For example, if your weekend included a story about **surfing**, and the person that you are talking to grew up in Hawaii and surfed every weekend – you're now in instant friend mode.

They will make positive assumptions about you – what do surfers have in common? No longer are you a stranger, but you are similar to them in many ways. This feeling of similarity and warmth only grows deeper with the more commonality that you include in your story.

It's not always possible to connect on such a deep level on specific topics, but relatability also means **not** telling stories about subjects or activities that no one cares about or has any knowledge about. That is the more important part.

It is one thing to have a funny story in your mind or a story that you think is funny. It's another to be actually ready to tell that story in a funny and entertaining way.

How do you fix this situation? Practice.

In fact, by practicing your story in front of a mirror or to yourself, you can see where you can **tweak your delivery** or maybe make some changes to make sure that the story is actually what it should be. In other words, if you're trying to tell a funny story, that story better be funny. If you are trying to tell a scary or a curious story, that story better be curious. You find out in the worst possible way when you assume that a story is interesting, and then you fall flat on your face when telling that story to people who aren't impressed.

You have to practice telling your story in order to become a really good storyteller. Part of this comes from your comfort level. The more you tell a story either to yourself, a friend, or a lot of people, the more comfortable you are in telling that story. You make fewer mistakes in terms of timing. You're able to deliver the story or its punch line in such a way that it has the maximum effect.

Delivery is not just timing. You have to be conscious of the different elements that go into effective storytelling. You have to have the right vocal tone and the right body language to maximize effective delivery.

<u>Try this exercise.</u>

Think about common questions that you might be asked in a typical social setting. Prepare some short twenty-second stories that are related to those questions (**How are you, how was your weekend, and how is work?).** This will allow you to make a great impression when people ask you those questions. Make sure that they are entertaining, have a point and purpose, and are relatable to people.

Just as important, make sure you give yourself the time and the space to practice these mini twenty-second stories in front of the mirror. Pay attention to your body language, how fast you speak, your tone of voice, and be aware of the precise time to drop the punch line or deliver home the point of the story. Keep practicing until you are perfectly comfortable with your effectiveness.

10. Vocal tone and inflection > actual words.

It's very easy to get caught up in the power of body language when it comes to making instant connections. After all, people see you coming, your gestures and mannerisms and how you stand. You're like a walking billboard of either positivity and good feelings or negativity and discomfort. You can always control the signal that you send to other people so that they can form the right impressions about you.

With that said, you also have to pay attention to the other signals you are sending out. You're not just a walking collection of body language signals. You're not just communicating with people non-verbally with your mannerisms, gestures, and facial expressions.

You must also pay attention to your **tone of voice** because that is going to say a lot about how you are perceived.

You have to remember that most of the time *how* **you say something** is more important than what you have to say. While the content of your words means a lot, the way you say it means even more. Your tone of voice plays a big role in the overall message received.

<u>Consistency is key.</u>

Make sure that your choice of vocal tone is **consistent** with your body language and the intent of your words. This means you have to be mindful of how you position your body and what you are saying. They all have to flow together.

People do not like to be confused. People do not like an **awkward interplay** between what you're saying, your facial expressions, and what you're doing with your hands and feet. This makes them extremely uncomfortable, and it makes you seem as if you have something to hide or are untrustworthy. If you've ever felt that something was just off about someone you just met, it was probably because they were sending mixed messages with their signals.

Unfortunately, it's very easy to be misread if we are unaware of the subconscious signals we project through our body language and vocal tone.

<u>Sarcasm and humor.</u>

The interesting thing about humor is that, on the one hand, it can lead to a genuine personal bond between people. On the other hand, it can easily divide people.

The problem with humor is that it is so **personal**. When you tell a joke, what may be a "rolling on the floor laughing my ass off" funny to you might be as unfunny as kids dying in a school bus fire to someone else. You can't just assume that the stuff you think is awesomely funny is also funny to others. If you insist on having your way and pushing through with such a joke, you might just end up alienating your audience.

You can spare yourself from unnecessary drama by staying away from overly convoluted or complicated humor (**when you first meet, of course**). Also, you might want to stay away from edgy or highly sarcastic and possibly highly negative humor. Only when you become more **familiar** with your audience should you go there. Sure, you might be forgiven if you make one inappropriate joke, but if you keep making them, one after the other, you're venturing into dangerous territory.

When you tell a joke, and it doesn't go over well, that should be a signal to you that your brand of humor probably isn't your audience's brand of humor, and you should move on to a lower level and possibly less objectionable joke or set humor aside completely.

Remember, this is a book about making **great first impressions** – a big part of that is avoiding the missteps that most people make, and **playing at their level**.

No mo' monotone.

People who speak in one tone are boring and forgettable. When was the last time you spoke with somebody who had a **flat tone**? Chances are you don't remember that person.

Make sure you ask your friends if they've noticed that you tell stories in a monotone voice. Ask them if there are certain times you talk in a monotone. Make sure you recognize times when you slip into this tone of voice and arrest it.

When people hear you speak in monotone, they assume that you are boring, or have very few emotions. Even worse, if you react to someone's story or joke in monotone, they will think that you don't understand the emotions that they are trying to convey.

Mirror others.

People respond favorably to others like them. As much as we hate to admit it, we are looking for people who are like us. When you talk in such a way that you copy your audience's **rate and tone of speech**, you are instantly more likeable. Also, if you copy their **energy level** when you talk, you appear more similar to them, and they will be more open to you.

Of course, you shouldn't go overboard. You shouldn't go to extremes because if you do that, it will look as if you are mocking them.

Try this exercise.

Make a recording of yourself reading something. Did you like what you heard? It probably sounded far more **monotone and emotionless** than you thought would.

Now read the same passage again, and make it as **cartoonish**, emotional, and lively as possible. Modulate the tone of your voice, its volume and **exaggerate** the emotions in the text.

Notice the difference?

Obviously you won't be anything close to the second version when you talk to people in real life, but you should aim for that and realize how much more you can convey with just your vocal tonality. This is important because it warms up your vocal cords, and gets your voice used to expressing such tones – after a while, your expressive vocal tonality expression will become a part of your muscle memory.

The great thing about this exercise is that there is nobody around to judge you or make fun of you. Keep recording yourself until you like what you hear. Put yourself in the shoes of your potential audience. Are you conveying what you want to convey through your tone? Is it unmistakable, or is it too vague and forgettable? Keep practicing.

11. Ask for people's opinions and advice; gain likability.

On a fundamental level, human beings are **selfish** creatures. Even those who live their lives selflessly tend to think, speak and act in ways that always come back to one thing: personal **gratification**.

Whether we want to admit it or not, there is always that element of self-centeredness and self-absorption rooted in our cores. It comes from a biological need for self-preservation, which persists even in a world where our lives are no longer constantly in danger. So you might as well **accept** that we are all a little self-involved.

Instead of trying to deny it, we would all be better off **embracing** it.

You can use it to your advantage when it comes to establishing a quick rapport and connection with other people.

You want people to like you? Appeal to their **sense of self-importance**.

Ask for their advice and opinions in a **calculated** way to make them invest in you and connect.

<u>Questions only they can answer.</u>

If you truly want to endear yourself to people, you have to be willing to **dig deep**.

Anyone can answer questions about the **weather**, for instance, so you aren't tapping into that sense of self-importance by asking someone a question 100 other people on the street could answer.

You have to make your questions specific to the **expertise and interests** of the person you are talking to. The question must ultimately focus on them. Converse about topics they are passionate about; things that they feel they are experts in. This gives them a chance to shine and an opportunity to strut their stuff. On a **subconscious** level, they'll feel grateful to you for giving them an opportunity to stand out from the crowd and explain their nuanced views of the topic.

This feeling of gratitude is even more intense if there are a few other people around to witness their display of expertise.

<u>Targeted conversations impart validation and value.</u>

Everybody wants to feel smart and that they matter. At the very least, people want to feel **validated** for being who they are. When you ask people for their advice or opinion regarding a subject they feel only they can answer, they get that validation.

Why? Because they feel as though you have specifically asked them because you recognize their expertise. As a result, they will almost always take a liking to you and they will feel good just being around you.

They will think, "This person recognizes my **particular brand of genius and insight**, so I had better connect with them! They get me and hold me in high regard."

People like hearing their own voices.

Everybody has an opinion on just about everything.

The good news about opinions is that they are precisely that, opinions. They aren't facts. Facts have to be true for them to be valid.

Opinions can be all over the place. That's the great thing about asking people for their opinions; there's really **no right or wrong** answer. You're giving the person an opportunity to stand in the spotlight and gain attention in a way they can't screw up.

Everybody wins when you ask people for their opinion, as long as you do it right. The person giving you their opinion feels like a genius, simply because you approached them wanting that opinion. You open up the door for an involved conversation, and you are endeared to them for valuing their insight.

Asking people for their advice or opinion is one of the best ways you can build instant rapport and become likeable in the eyes of many people.

Try this exercise.

Hang out with a friend that you know well. List **5 topics** that you know they love talking about, whether it is an interest of theirs or their occupation.

Do a tiny bit of research and discover a popular debate or topic of conversation about each of those 5 topics. Now ask your friend to **elaborate** on each of the topics of conversation, and ask them for **actionable advice** if you can shoehorn it into the conversation.

Show a willingness and eagerness to hear from them. Encourage them at every pause and turn to continue.

Chances are that you won't have to encourage them – they'll relish the **opportunity** to talk about something they know so intimately, to someone that so obviously wants to learn about it. They'll explain each side of the argument, and debate with themselves over its merits. They'll make a ton of recommendations on how you should proceed, and practically fall over themselves to make sure that you have the proper resources at your command.

12. People like similarity.

As much as we would like to **think** that we are open-minded and can get along with people from every background and origin, the reality is that we get along best with people who we think are like us. In fact, we seek them out.

It's why Little Italy, Chinatown, and Koreatown exist.

But I'm not just talking about race, skin color, religion, or sexual orientation. I'm talking about people who share our values, look at the world the same way we do, and have the same take on things as we do.

We tend to gravitate toward those people regardless of what they look like, where they come from, what accents they may have, or their sexual orientation. As the old saying goes, birds of a feather flock together.

This is a very **common human tendency** that is rooted in how our species developed. Imagine this: you are walking in a wasteland thousands of years ago and you're out with people who have very different values from you. If you hang out with people who want to do what you want to do, chances are you will do it. Chances are you will meet with success.

We're looking for familiarity and for people who share our goals towards a common objective. You can use this to your advantage in the here and now in your efforts to make instant connections and boost your likeability.

Here are some considerations to keep in mind so you can craft a strategy to make this basic truth about human nature work for you.

<u>Dig for similar perspectives, negative and positive.</u>

There are a lot of apathetic people out there, but there are some **hot-button issues** that you'll find nearly everyone and their mother has an opinion about.

One of the best ways to dig for similarities with other (new) people is to talk about these hot-button issues and find out exactly where they stand on them. You can see immediately where you can seize upon a similarity and **bond instantly** over it.

Do they share a particular like or dislike for something? Is there something they said that you vehemently agree or disagree with?

It's something you can share, it's something you can both feel good about and something you can bond over. Keep in mind that this topic can be negative or positive. Don't think that the topic itself has to be positive or wholesome or politically correct. As long as it's a topic that both of you

sincerely agree on, you can both feel great talking about that particular topic and it can bond you.

<u>Mutual hate is just as good as mutual love - plus, it's more fun.</u>

Have you noticed that when you're talking to certain people who share certain interests with you, the topic will often veer to a **subtopic** that you both hate? You both dislike a particular situation or person.

Many people think this is a negative thing. Many people think it would be best to back off, and not indulge in a **hatefest of negativity**.

Actually, this makes for a great bonding moment because just as common love for a subject is a great way to bond, so is **common dislike**. In fact, hate regarding a particular topic leads to a deeper feeling of shared ideas. This is where you see eye to eye. This is where you realize that you're on the same page. This can lead to a feeling that you are fun to be around.

How many friendships have been built in army boot camps, where the singular common bond was a hatred for the suffering they are going through? How many friendships have been built on the back of hating the same teacher or morning schedule?

<u>Maximize shared moments.</u>

When on you focus on the things you both agree on, and it's obvious that you have a similar take on many different topics in life, this can lead to a feeling of a **shared moment**.

The impression that you have a shared moment really goes a long way toward intimate sharing.

You have to remember that the world can be a lonely place. People often feel alone and as though nobody really understands them. The minute you are able to get them to realize that you share this deep personal moment with them, the more they will like you. The more they will feel like "**Wow! This person truly gets me**" or at least, "This person gets one part of me."

This can lead to **inside jokes and references** that only they will get. The more you do this, the more people will stop looking at you as a stranger and start looking at you as somebody who is close to who they are. That is precisely where you want to be, in terms of instant likeability and instant connections.

Try this exercise.

Imagine two concepts that you really despise. It could be people, places, or things. The more **obscure and specific** the better.

Now imagine that you've met someone who happens to hate the **exact same obscure thing** that you do!

This person has also been to Pennsylvania, seen that particular intersection, been fooled by that hidden STOP sign and been pulled over by the same hillbilly police officer that has a huge mole on his right cheek...and the mole reminded both of you of Elvis Presley?

Well, you've got a lot to talk about with that person, don't you?

In this way you can see exactly how little loves and hates can completely bond us to other people.

13. Listening is likable.

If there's any one principle you need to wrap your mind around when it comes to your listening skills, it is this: **it is not about you**.

Realize everyone in the world thinks that the universe revolves around them. If the human species has survived this long, it's because of its **profound self-interest**. We have self-preservation, self-absorption, self-reflection, and self-interest hard wired into our brains. If we didn't, our species wouldn't have survived this long.

We now have the **luxury** of stepping outside of our self-interest. Unfortunately, not enough people do it, and this is precisely why listening skills are so bad in this day and age. If you want to be likeable, you have to have **strong listening skills**.

The good news is that it's easier than you think. It only involves temporarily **turning off** the tendency to focus on yourself and hear yourself talk. Instead, turn your attention to the person in front of you.

By realizing that the conversation is not about you, you give yourself permission to be truly curious and interested in what the other person is saying.

People aren't dumb. People can detect when you are **truly engaged and interested** in what they have to say. When they see enough of the right signals, the more they will talk, and more important, the more they'll like you. That's how it works. Here are some tips to maximize your listening skills by focusing on this fundamental strategy of turning away from self-focus to focusing on others.

Stop talking and start asking.

It's very hard to learn when you are **not listening**.

You start **learning** when you stop talking. You increase your rate of learning when you start asking questions and directing the questions to gaps in your knowledge.

Think of effective listening this way: it's a way to bridge gaps in your understanding regarding a particular subject matter – **the other person**.

Listening to others is actually one of the most self-interested things you can do. Because the only person that truly benefits when you stop talking and start asking questions is **you**. Your understanding regarding a particular subject matter becomes more complete, you become more knowledgeable, and the next time you talk to somebody you have a little bit more to offer. It's a complete **win-win** situation.

Unfortunately, people don't see things this way. Most people would rather hear themselves talk. In many cases, people aren't really interested in what other people have to say.

One of the best things about improving your listening skills is that it benefits **you** tremendously. And I'm not just talking about appearing more likeable. I'm talking about effectively becoming a better and more informed person.

Master active listening.

Chances are you've probably heard of the phrase "active listening". You've probably heard it so many times, but don't even know what it means. Active listening is simply all about being in control of how you listen.

Passive listening is basically just leaning back, letting the other person talk, and saying "uh-huh, uh-huh", or "go on, go on." If that's how you listen, congratulations. You are just like everybody else.

Active listening, on the other hand, involves a focus; it involves a **strategy**. Active listening is all about paying attention to what the other person is saying and categorizing that information. If there's a missing category, or if there is a certain break in the logic of what that person is saying, you then follow up to bridge those gaps.

When people talk, they usually make **claims**. For example, somebody says, "Dave is a great worker." Usually, you would expect, when somebody makes a claim like that, that they will share evidence or facts that will support their statement. When evidence is missing, that's when active listening should kick in.

That's when you should ask, "Why is that?" Or you could ask comparison questions.

The questioning should lead to the **information that is missing** that will support a claim. That is what separates active listening from passive listening. Passive listening is really just giving the other person a forum and letting them run their mouth. Active listening is a form of listening that clues the other person to the fact that you're truly monitoring the conversation, and you are calling them into account regarding what they're saying.

People appreciate active listeners because active listeners keep them on their toes; active listeners actually challenge them to present information in a more informative way. Most people appreciate active listeners. With passive listening, on the other hand, it's very easy to confuse your passive listening style with the listening pattern of a person who doesn't care.

Shine the spotlight on other people.

By actively listening to another person, you focus the spotlight on them. You stop talking, and you ask them questions that make them feel **validated**. They feel that they are the center of the show. They feel that all your attention is focused on them. The more questions you ask, the more they feel validated.

At a minimum, your questions should illuminate or

elaborate on what they are saying. A key part of doing this is to repeat the last three words of what they said to lead to a question or, at the very least, to get them to keep talking.

The whole point of improving your listening skills is to draw the other person out. Let them talk about what's important to them. Let them take center stage.

<u>Try this exercise.</u>

In front of a mirror, practice saying phrases like "go on", "and then", "why?", and make sure that your facial expressions reflect genuine interest.

Next, talk to your friends and practice these phrases. You will realize that there are certain similar or equivalent phrases besides these; go ahead and practice those. Make it your goal to have the other person keep talking, and see if you can make a conversation entirely about learning about them. Try to speak as little as possible, and learn as much as you can about whatever the other person wants to talk about.

Pay attention to the logic of what they're saying and quickly analyze if there are gaps in their story or their narrative. Ask questions regarding those gaps and then tie that in to what they said earlier. The more you do this, the more engaged everyone becomes.

14. Read hints, cues, and clues.

The interesting thing about interacting with human beings is that we're always talking. always communicating with each other. For the most part, we are not using words. We are using all sorts of signals that aren't tied to the actual words we use to communicate.

For example "**dude**" in American parlance can be vocalized in the form of a question, surprise, to express camaraderie, disgust, fear, or admiration.

The funny thing is "dude" is just one of the long list of words that you can vocalize in a certain way to fit a certain set of circumstances that trigger **specific emotional responses**. How can we tell which emotion is to be evoked?

We communicate with our facial expressions, tone of voice, and body language. If you want to be instantly likeable, you can't just focus on the words that come out of people's minds. If you do that you will be missing a lot of the messages people send your way – in other words, what people are really trying to say to you.

Sensory cues.

Sensory cues involve your **perception**; when you smell something, when you touch somebody, when you hear somebody, when you see somebody. These are all sensory cues. When people do something that seems like it **impacts their senses**, it's a hint about what they truly feel. Of course, there's a danger that you will read too much into this. But you should at least look at it as some sort of signal for you to dig even deeper and find other supporting signals to help you truly understand what the person is communicating.

One common example of a sensory signal people give when they are taken aback, or shocked, or even made uncomfortable, is when you walk into a room wearing a very loud shirt and **people rub their eyes**. This is completely non verbal. This is completely based on their sense of sight. This shows that your outfit threw them off.

You might want to pay attention to what you're wearing. Or you might want to diffuse the situation by making jokes about what you're wearing. Either way, this is a signal to you that they have an issue with what you're wearing.

Similarly, if you say something, and somebody **pinches or wrinkles their nose**, this is an involuntary signal to you that they found something "stinky" or disagreeable about something you shared.

If something is too **loud** or they simply don't want to hear it, they will cover their face, ears, or clench their teeth. If something tastes too **sour** or they don't like the feeling that it evokes it, we make a pained face and smack our mouths.

If something is too **hot** to touch or causes some kind of emotional pain, we clench our hand and attempt to shake the pain off.

Essentially, the ways that you might react to a **physical sensation** can also be present in how people react to verbal and non-verbal signals from others. Pay attention!

1. Body language.
    1.1. Are they facing you or slightly turned away? Indicates disinterest or discomfort.
    1.2. What directions are their feet facing? Indicates whether they want to keep talking to you or leave.
    1.3. Are they fidgeting or do they appear antsy otherwise? Indicates discomfort or anxiety.
    1.4. Are their arms and legs crossed, or uncrossed and more open and inviting? Indicates how comfortable and open they feel to you.
    1.5. Is their posture slumped over or more horizontal than vertical? Indicates boredom or disinterest.
    1.6. Are they using quick, decisive gestures? Indicates anger or annoyance.
    1.7. Are they touching you? Indicates comfort and affection.
2. Eyes.
    2.1. Are they making eye contact with you or scanning in back of you? Indicates boredom.
    2.2. Are they avoiding eye contact with you? Indicates boredom or possible dislike.
    2.3. Are they staring at you? Indicates possible confrontation, anxiety, or boredom.
3. Distance.

3.1. Are they standing close to you? Indicates comfort.

3.2. Are they moving farther away every time you move close? Indicates discomfort.

4. Facial expressions.

    4.1. Are they squinting at you? Indicates skepticism or annoyance.

    4.2. Can you see micro-expressions form before they can hide them?

    4.3. Are their eyebrows shooting up? Indicates surprise or happiness.

    4.4. Are their smiles fake or genuine? You can tell this by how much their eyes crinkle, and if they show their teeth.

    4.5. Are they rolling their eyes at you? Indicates skepticism and annoyance.

5. Verbal cues.

    5.1. Are they acknowledging what you're saying, or just giving you "Uh huh"s?

    5.2. Are they using rising vocal tone and inflection? Indicates confusion or anger.

    5.3. Are they stuttering or stumbling over how to address something? Indicates nervousness or disinterest in a topic.

    5.4. Are they laughing or giggling at what you say? Indicates affection.

    5.5. Do they keep asking questions? Indicates interest.

6. Other behaviors.

    6.1. Are they checking their phone a lot? Indicates boredom.

    6.2. Did they excuse themselves quickly after beginning to talk to you? Indicates dislike.

    6.3. Do they continually refer to other things they have to be doing? Indicates anxiety and boredom.

The whole point of learning how to read verbal and non-verbal clues people give off is to give you feedback regarding your ability to hold and manage a conversation. You have to remember that in order to maximize your likeability and ability to establish instant rapport with people you have to process and interpret these individual signals.

Try this exercise.

When you yourself want to stop talking to someone, what do you do? Imagine that you have been accosted by the most annoying person that you know. But, they are your boss's good friend. You cannot afford to be anything other than nice to this person, but you can't stand them.

How do you demonstrate that you want to stop talking to them? How do you subtly send them signs that you are not interested in the conversation?

How do you behave in such a way that they leave on their own?

Is it a combination of short replies, a lack of eye contact, or excuses? Do you turn your feet away from them?

Now you know what to look for in other people!

15. Go with the flow; don't derail the train.

I've already gone to some length regarding the secret to becoming an effective listener. It's simple: **focus on the other person**.

When you stop talking, shut up, and start opening your ears to what the other person has to say, you instantly become a genius to them.

You're just taking advantage of a key fact of human nature. We want the attention to be focused on **us**. When we're talking to somebody who seems **genuinely** engaged in our conversation and likes to listen to us talk, we can't help but like that person.

One key aspect of becoming an effective conversationalist, and using that skill to build effective rapport, is to go with the flow of the conversation. If you constantly interject, define, correct, or go off on tangents that don't pertain to the topic at hand, you cut the conversation **off at the legs**.

Look at a conversation like a **steam train**. It takes that kind of train a while to pick up **momentum** and really hit its stride. But every tangent or point where you say "Actually, that's not right…" serves to hit the **brakes** on the conversational steam train. You'll never be able to get deep into any topic; you will just stay at a speed that people can **speedwalk** faster than.

Remember the end goal: to make a great impression and connect with people. It's not to make sure people know that we know everything there is to know about Star Wars, or correct their understanding of World War II. The interaction isn't about you **showcasing** your knowledge, which inevitably makes a poor impression.

These things are firmly outside the flow of a conversation. Like the steam train, it's like accelerating and then hitting the brakes immediately. It's a stop and go conversation, and you never give a connection a chance to develop if you are constantly derailing the train and hitting the brakes. You can never get deep into any one topic, and we know that that's the baseline for building a connection.

Don't be a pedant.

First of all, resist all urges to be a **pedant**.

A pedant is someone who is **highly-detailed oriented**, usually in an annoying way. People hate pedants.

Pedants make a big deal out of the small stuff in a conversation and they hammer small details to the ground, while **ignoring** the actual points being made.

They **divert attention** to things that don't matter in the name of being correct about something. If you are a pedant, you are going to be as fun to talk to as having hemorrhoid surgery.

Let's say that you have an objectively kickass story about your weekend involving **snowboarding**.

Here's what a pedant will do: ask about the model of your snowboard, and tell you the history of the company that made it. Then, they will make clear the angles of the slopes. Then, they will correct you and explain why you were incorrect about the seasons with the best snow.

Do you find yourself interjecting "**Actually…!**" in conversations often? Then you might be a pedant.

Pedants focus so much on the specific **trees** that they miss the whole **forest**. And in the vast majority of cases, no one really cares about the trees. A story is told to deliver an **overall message or experience**, not to expound on specific details.

When you ask questions that are not relevant to the main message of experience, you introduce a verbal **red light** and stop the sharing.

The whole point of engaging people in a conversation is to draw them out of their shells. You're not giving them that opportunity when you're putting a stoplight in front of their faces by being pedantic.

Pedants often feel the need to do what they do because they want to show their knowledge on a particular topic. Digging deeper, it's actually a base **insecurity** about what they feel they can contribute to a conversation. They may not be able to contribute an enthralling story like their friends, but at least they can contribute some noise by pouncing on something they can correct or talk about in detail ... often unrelated to the point at hand.

Accordingly, if you **acknowledge their knowledge or contributions** to a conversation, they can feel much better about themselves and stop pedantically interrupting you as much.

Don't correct people all the time.

Closely related to pedantry is the need to correct others. If you correct others on small, **inconsequential details** when they are telling a story, you will just annoy them.

Again, it completely destroys the flow of a conversation if you focus on something that isn't important to the main point, and it only serves to showcase some knowledge that you have.

It is even worse if you do this when you're **arguing** with someone, as it can be perceived as you avoiding or diverting issues so you don't have to take **blame**.

"Why can't you wash the dishes more?"
"Actually, one of those spoons is yours."

Is that the point that's trying to be made? Can you imagine how infuriating a response that would be?

Little white lies.

As you might reckon, keeping the flow of a conversation can sometimes mean **glazing over** the little details so you can actually reach the main message that someone is trying to convey.

And yes, sometimes this might involve **feigning knowledge or ignorance** of a certain subject so that you can further the ultimate goal – conversational flow and connection.

One basic example is when the person you're talking with references a **commercial**.

The commercial represents something that they like, or is used to prove a point – that's why they inserted it in the conversation. What the commercial is about has literally zero relevance; if you can glean the meaning of the commercial, that's what matters. No need to interrupt and ask about the commercial.

The interesting or important part is not the commercial itself. The interesting thing is that they are referring to the commercial as part of a joke or a story. The focus is on the joke or story. *Not the commercial.*

So, if you want to categorize this as a **white lie,** file it away under the "**your baby IS actually cute**" category. It's a **necessary evil** to keep flow and good relations.

The bottom line is this: if you don't know something specific but can readily understand the prevailing message and purpose of it in a story or statement, then just go along. It keeps a conversation flowing, trim, and on point.

<u>Laugh at yourself.</u>

When people joke with you and poke fun at you, learn to laugh at yourself.

When you take **offense** or when you become **defensive**, that is a stoplight for the conversation and the very opposite of conversational flow. It doesn't matter that you were not the one who introduced the potential roadblock – it is still your duty to make a conversation not stop abruptly.

You have to remember that the vast majority of people **respect** you and **care** about you. They are poking fun at you precisely because they feel that you can take it, and that your relationship is strong enough for it. Of course... if you feel that something is borne out of disrespect, this is a completely different piece of advice.

But 99% of the time, people don't mean anything malicious by their jokes, and just want to banter with you. **Indulge them (if they haven't crossed boundaries)**!

So as much as possible, learn to laugh at yourself. Don't be so **thin-skinned** that every little detail is offensive. Dish it back to them in a joking manner.

You don't want to be the type of person who people feel that they have to **walk on eggshells** around – this makes everyone self-conscious and is like salting the dirt of a garden: say goodbye to any chances of organic connection.

This entire chapter underscores the following: people think

that conversational chemistry is just non-stop, flowing banter; the kind without any silences, the kind that flows easily from topic to topic. And most importantly, the kind without interruptions and interjections that lead nowhere.

So focus on the overall flow of a conversation and give the other person what they will perceive a genuine connection looks like!

Try this exercise.

Ask a friend to tell you about their weekend in one sentence. That should get the main point of their weekend to you neatly. Don't interrupt them, and just listen to their one sentence.

Now ask them to tell you that same weekend in eight sentences. This may not be easy to stretch a weekend into eight sentences, but the point is to make them dig for details and information that they wouldn't have unearthed otherwise.

Now after you hear their eight sentences, ask them five questions. The catch is this: all of the questions have to relate to the main thrust of the story you should have gotten from the one sentence description, but integrate details from the eight sentence story.

Do you see what we are doing here? You are making sure that you can **identify** and stick with the **main flow** of a conversation, even with an abundance of other details that may or may not be relevant. This will teach you to focus on the main message someone wants to present, and how to continue talking about *it* as opposed to irrelevant details.

16. Genuine, real expressions.

People like **honesty**.

I need to point out the obvious because people take it for granted, especially in social interactions.

This isn't a moral stand or anything, it's just that when people feel that others are being dishonest or less than genuine, it leaves a spectacularly bad taste in their mouths.

Okay, so what do we do with this knowledge?

People love genuineness and honesty, so give it to them. You will be able to establish connections more easily.

That's a loaded statement – how exactly do you give people genuineness and honesty aside from just not lying to them?

Genuine smiles.

Let's get this clear up front: there are **two types of smiles** – fake and real. There are no in-betweens.

It's exceedingly easy for me to tell the difference between

the two, so let me share the following tips. There are **three things** to look for when evaluating when someone actually is smiling at your joke and presence genuinely, or simply putting on a show for social grace's sake.

First, a real smile will cause someone's eyes to wrinkle and squint. Their eyes won't be 100% open, and this will cause their forehead to wrinkle as well. If someone's eyes are expressionless, despite their mouths appearing to smile, it is not a genuine smile and it is meant to disguise what that person is really feeling. In a sense, it's a **mask**!

If you think you're pulling something off and fooling the other person, think again. People aren't dumb. They can tell a genuine smile from a not-so-genuine smile. People can tell when you're just trying to be polite, and when you are actually engaged and truly interested in what they have to say and who they are.

Second, show your teeth!

One of the worst ways to smile is to smile with tight and closed lips. It's as if somebody is basically forcing your face upward to give off an impression that somewhat looks like a smile. It looks almost like you're being tortured, or you just swallowed something very bitter or something that tastes really nasty. It comes off as fake and, more important, it can put people off. If you're trying to impress people, if you're trying to establish rapport where people feel good around you, stay away from tight-lipped smiles.

Third, real smiles don't fade immediately after a punchline hits. They linger on a person's face, eyes and mouth – and then their face slowly returns to a blank slate. If someone's smile fades too quickly and the joy is wiped from their face, you have a fake smile in front of you!

If you want to be more genuine in the smiles you give to people, you have to master the physical signals.

Your **whole face** must change when you smile. Nothing is more robotic than when you just open your mouth and show teeth, or you just move your lips upward but there's no teeth showing. That's not a genuine smile. People can tell a mile away, and they will make an instant judgment regarding how friendly you truly are.

The best way to do this is to stand in front of a mirror, and practice how you normally smile.

Now, with **utter objectivity**, look at the smile that you're giving yourself. Put yourself in another person's shoes. Would you be impressed or fooled? Would you think that that smile is genuine? Now start making changes with the other parts of your face and see how that feels. Smile without moving your eyes; then smile without opening your mouth.

Next, talk to a friend and show them your **facial expressions** and ask for their feedback. You will hear if what you're doing truly registers or if it appears fake.

Genuine laughter.

Real laughter is also not forced... and is easy to distinguish.

With few exceptions, real laughter comes from the belly and is often uncontrollable. If your laughter comes off as fake, instead of others liking you, they will feel that you are **pandering** to them and deceiving them.

Fake laughter makes people **uneasy**. Fake laughter actually makes people feel that you're laughing at them instead of at their joke. To avoid all that unnecessary drama, you need to think about what your real and fake laughs sound like. Notice the vocal tone and volume of your laugh. Know what separates genuine laughter from fake or forced laughter so you can spot it in others as well.

Distinguish sarcasm from genuine interest.

This is important, because much of the time, sarcasm and genuine interest can sound **identical**.

A continuing lack of clarity can make people extremely uncomfortable.

There are two ways to transform a potentially sarcastic statement into a genuine statement of positivity.

First, you explicitly say that you're not being sarcastic, and that you genuinely feel that way. This tackles the lack of clarity head-on, and leaves no room for misunderstanding.

Second, you simply make sure that all of your signs – your vocal tone, words, intent, facial expression and body language – are consistent with one another.

The next time you are talking to a friend, pay attention to

their tone of voice. Notice when they are excited about something, notice when they are truly engaged. Pay attention to their reactions. Much of social skill development is observation – knowing exactly what to look for, and integrating that information into your own habits.

People hate dishonesty. So stay away from any kind of expression that makes you look less than genuine. I'm not saying that there's a one-size-fits-all formula for being genuine, but by paying attention to patterns, you can see what works and what doesn't work.

Try this exercise.

Compare pictures of yourself taken when you know you were genuinely smiling, to a picture of yourself when you smiled only with your mouth (and by not moving your eyes). Next, compare that genuine smile picture to a picture when you intentionally kept your mouth closed.

What's the difference? Does one look **faker** than the other? Which looks **friendlier** and more **natural**?

These can be small, subtle differences, but people pick up on these more easily than you might think.

Conclusion

The first 60 seconds are the gatekeeper to everything that you want in life, I hope that much is clear to you now.

Learn to master it, and you give yourself a fighting chance to connect with anyone. Life isn't who you know, it's who you connect with.

Techniques and tactics are important, as are best practices in opening people up to you, but the most important part is the attitude that you bring to every interaction that immediately sets the tone.

Curiosity, helpfulness, and genuineness will take you much farther than a set of icebreaker questions in your back pocket.

Sincerely,

Patrick King
Dating and Social Skills Coach
www.PatrickKingConsulting.com

P.S. If you enjoyed this book, please don't be shy and drop

me a line, leave a review, or both! I love reading feedback, and reviews are the lifeblood of Kindle books, so they are always welcome and greatly appreciated.

<u>Other books by Patrick King include:</u>

CHATTER: Small Talk, Charisma, and How to Talk to Anyone http://www.amazon.com/dp/B00J5HH2Y6

Cheat sheet

1. 60 seconds to everything you want in life. The first few seconds of any interaction with new people is key because it determines how invested people decide they want to be with you. If you fall on the negative end of the spectrum too often, you're going to have problems in life.

2. So what drives instant rapport and connection? Put simply, people want to connect with others because we are social creatures. Usually rapport is built by luck and chance, but training yourself to find commonalities anywhere builds instant rapport.

3. Best attitudes and practices to click instantly. Visualize that new people can all teach you something, and you're curious about them. Do NOT visualize that they represent goals for you, and can be used in other ways for your own benefit.

4. What first impression are you sending out? Be aware and observe the verbal and non-verbal signals that you are sending out to others, and how they will be perceived. Optimize your first impression for snap judgments.

5. Inbound and outbound positivity. If you embody positivity, praises, and compliments to others generously, it

will come back to you. It will influence interactions and immediately warm people to you.

6. Zero effort, small acts of service endear people to you. The small things matter and add up to an overall perception of you. If you simply perform acts of service for others, most of which are no effort to you, you will be viewed amazingly positively.

7. People bond through their imperfections; perfection is uncomfortable. Don't worry about hiding your flaws, because that makes people uncomfortable around you. People also embrace and bond through flaws and imperfections, so trying to be perfect is always a mistake.

8. Open and friendly body language is as important as your words. Your words are a minority of the message that you send to others, so your body language is important to be aware of and master. Many people's default body language is cold and standoffish, so combat that.

9. Prepare to click with rehearsed stories. Conversations follow typical patterns with typical openers and questions. Recognize which ones will occur in your daily life and prepare stories for them designed to be relatable and interesting.

10. Vocal tone and inflection > actual words. No monotone vocal tones, be careful on your sarcasm and humor differentiations, and mirror your conversation partner's vocal mannerisms.

11. Ask for people's opinions and advice; gain likability. If you can make someone feel special by asking for their personalized thoughts on something they have expertise in,

they will perceive you to be smart and similar to them.

12. People like similarity. Shared moments, whether negative or positive, are strong jumping points for conversation and connection. Negative ones might be more fruitful, even.

13. Listening is likable. Allow other people to step onto their soapbox and learn all that you can from them by showing an intense interest in them and listening.

14. Read hints, cues, and clues. Social cues and sensory cues are ways that you can figure out what someone really means, and not just what they say.

15. Go with the flow; don't derail the train. The greater goal of a conversation is usually flow and banter, as opposed to details, exactness, and corrections.

16. Genuine, real expressions. Real and fake smiles (and other expressions of emotion) are surprisingly easy to distinguish if you know what to look for – recognize the signs in others so you can tell what people are really thinking, and know how to make yourself appear genuine.

Made in the USA
San Bernardino, CA
26 July 2016